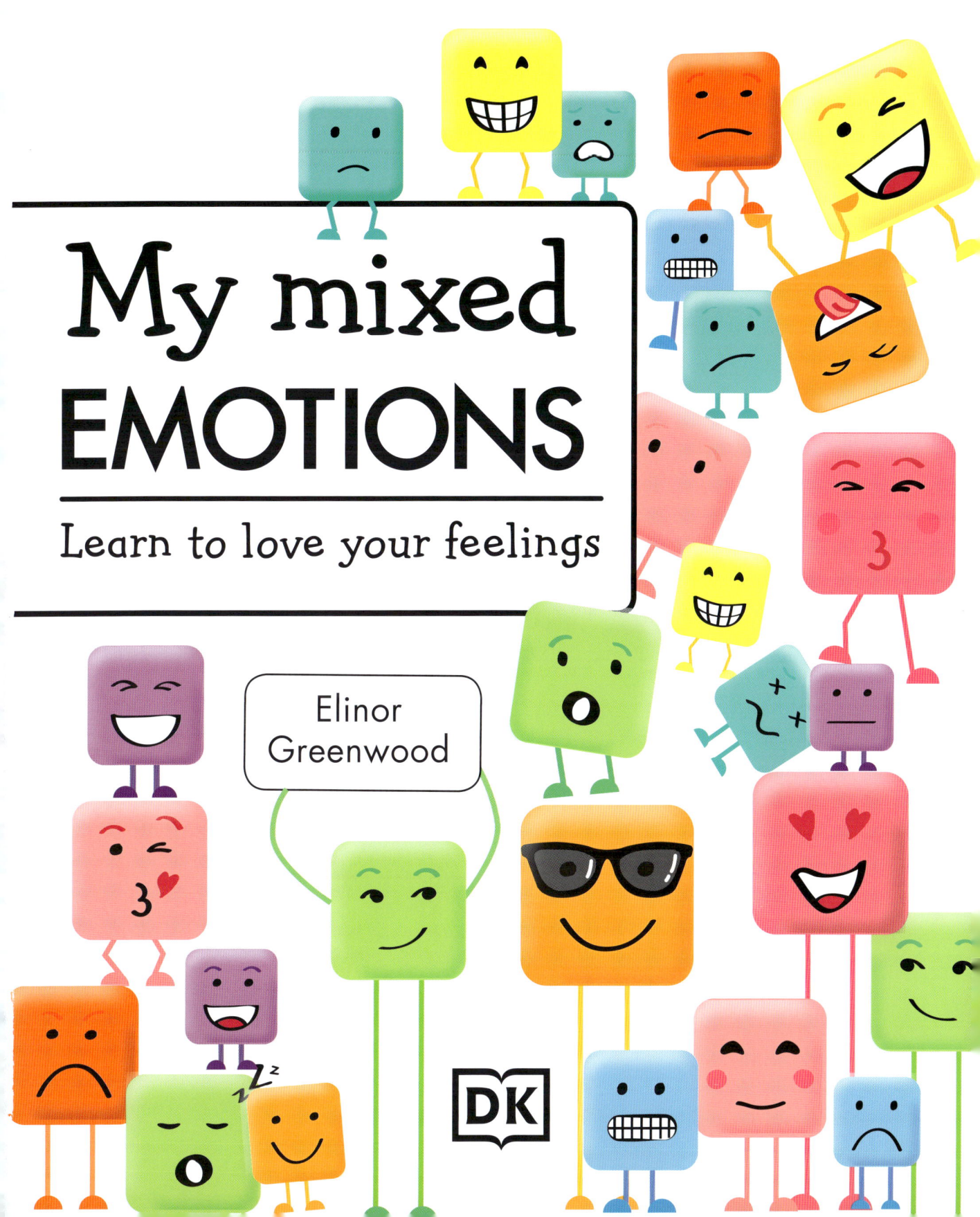

My mixed
EMOTIONS

Learn to love your feelings

Elinor
Greenwood

DK

Written by Elinor Greenwood
Editor Violet Peto
Art Editor Claire Patané
Project Art Editor and Illustrator Polly Appleton
Additional Illustration Charlotte Milner, Amy Keast
Design Assistance Charlotte Bull, Eleanor Bates
Child Psychology Consultant Maureen Healy
Science Consultant Wendy Horobin
Senior Producer, Pre-Production Nikoleta Parasaki
Senior Producer Amy Knight
Jacket Designer Claire Patané
Jacket Co-ordinator Francesca Young
Managing Editor Penny Smith
Managing Art Editor Mabel Chan
Publisher Mary Ling
Art Director Jane Bull

First published in Great Britain in 2018 by
Dorling Kindersley Limited
20 Vauxhall Bridge Road,
London, SW1V 2SA

The authorised representative in the EEA is
Dorling Kindersley Verlag GmbH. Arnulfstr. 124,
80636 Munich, Germany

Copyright © 2018 Dorling Kindersley Limited
A Penguin Random House Company
10 9
047–308912–Aug/18

A CIP catalogue record for this book
is available from the British Library.
ISBN: 978-0-2413-2376-2

Printed and bound in China

www.dk.com

This book was made with Forest
Stewardship Council™ certified
paper – one small step in DK's
commitment to a sustainable future.
For more information go to
www.dk.com/our-green-pledge

Introduction

Feeling Happy

Feeling Angry

Feeling Fear

Feeling Sad

The wonder of You

Contents

5   A note for grown-ups
6   Meet the emotions
8   The emotions HQ

10   What a feeling!
12   All are important

14   All about happiness
16   Happy ever after
18   A bowl of happiness
20   Be grateful

22   ...especially for you!
24   Chill-out time
26   Relax, relax
28   Have a mindful day

30   All about anger
32   Seeing red
34   Anger issues
36   That's not fair!

38   Let it go
40   Green-eyed monster
42   Call the jealousy doctor!

44   All about fear
46   It's hair-raising!
48   What to do about worrying
50   A new beginning

52   What to do when you're NEW
54   Separation and divorce
56   I have two homes now

58   All about sadness
60   Good grief
62   Beat the blues
64   Bullying fact file

66   How to handle bullying
68   I don't fit in!
70   Why do pets die?

72   The wonder of you
74   I'm the best me there is
76   You can do it!

78   My emotions dictionary
79   Glossary
80   Index/Acknowledgements

Calm is a super power!

Place 2 Be

It is all too easy to overlook the emotions of children, to assume that their hopes, fears, and dreams are somehow not as all-encompassing as those of adults. But that is not the case. Children feel things intensely. Three children in every classroom have a diagnosable mental health problem so giving children support early in their lives is crucial.

We all need good mental health to engage positively with our lives and develop the resilience to cope with life's problems. Recognizing our feelings, talking about them, and seeking support are life skills that help us into adulthood. They underpin successful relationships, engagement with learning, and ultimately help us develop into flourishing adults who can face the world with a sense of confidence and self-belief.

At Place2Be we provide school-based support and in-depth training programmes to improve the emotional well-being of pupils, families, teachers, and school staff. We reach more than 126,000 children each year, encouraging them to talk about their feelings on issues as diverse as friendships, bullying, family breakdown, and bereavement.

It is never too early to start talking about emotions with children and this book is a wonderful place to start.

Dame Benny Refson, DBE
President and founder, Place2Be

To find out more about Place2Be's work, or to support us, visit www.place2be.org.uk

Getting professional help

Occasionally children may need professional help. Each child is different and sometimes there are no easy answers. If you are worried, visit your GP or arrange a consultation with your child's school. They will be able to point you in the right direction according to the individual needs of your child. Here are some national contacts:

* Youngminds.org.uk has a freephone parents' helpline: 0808 802 5544

* Childline has a 24 hour helpline: 0800 1111

* This NHS Choices webpage has all the mental health helplines listed http://www.nhs.uk/Conditions/stress-anxiety-depression/Pages/mental-health-helplines

Meet the **emotions**

Excited

Nervous

Hello, great to meet you! How are you **feeling** today?

Feelings affect every part of everyone's life every day...

...so it's good to find out about them.

Shy

Joyful

Embarrassed

Loving

Disgusted

Calm

Trusting

6

Here are four of the really BIG ONES.

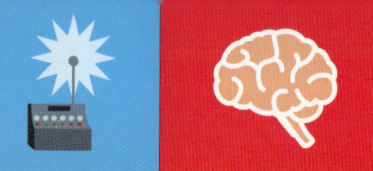

The **emotions** HQ

Feelings and **emotions** begin deep inside your **brain.** **From there**, they can affect every part of you, from your head to your toes.

Here's how your brain reacts to something scary or dangerous.

Emotions are made here!

Prefrontal cortex

Hypothalamus

Thalamus

Hippocampus

1 Your **eyes** see a **huge spider.**

2 Like a giant switchboard, your **thalamus** directs the information from your eyes to other parts of the **brain.**

8

Emotions are complex, but your brain can sort them out!

3

Your **hippocampus** makes the decision – **this is scary!**

?

4

Your **prefrontal cortex** releases chemicals to make you **react** to the threat.

AAAH!

5

The **hypothalamus** is responsible for activating the alarm response. Messages are sent to release **stress hormones.** Now you run away!

Run away!

All this happens in a tenth of a second!

00:00 10

Emotions move you to react quickly.

Did you know that sometimes your body responds faster to your basic emotions than your thoughts? You can look out for tell-tale signs you are becoming emotional, like tense neck, jaw, shoulders, arms, hands, or chest. Then try and change the situation.

What a feeling!

Look at these pictures of a **human body.** In a study, this is where people said they **feel** the different **emotions.**

Disgust

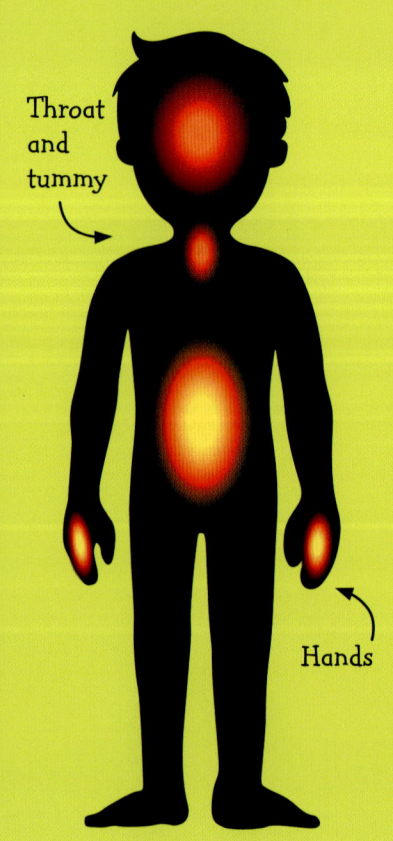

Throat and tummy

Hands

Happiness

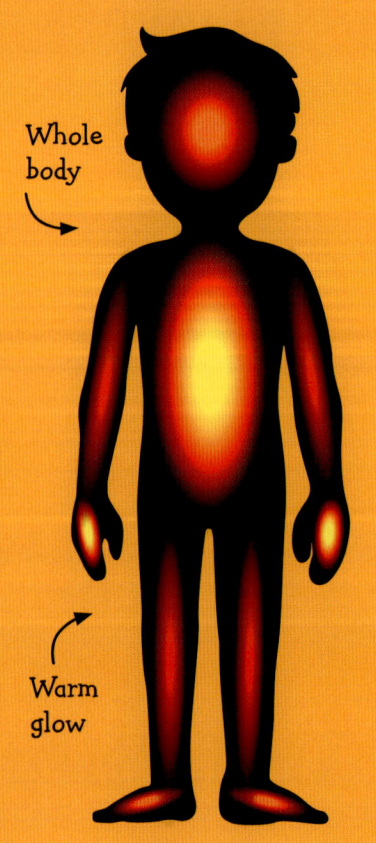

Whole body

Warm glow

Anger

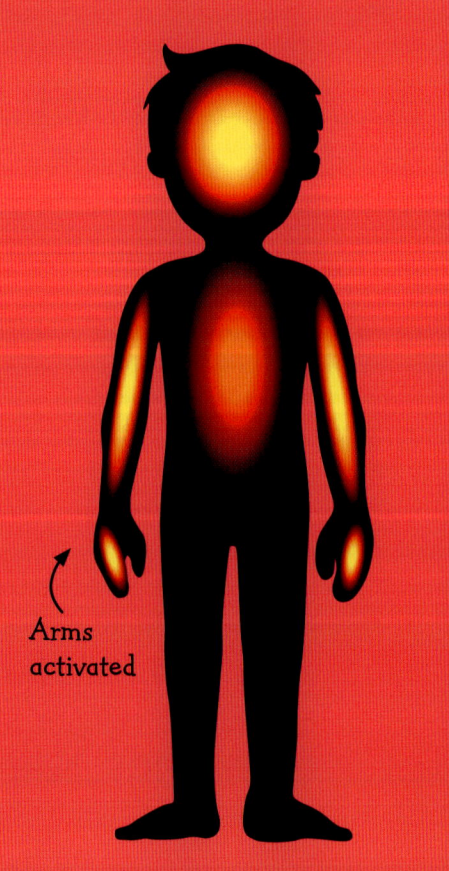

Arms activated

Do you agree?

Draw out some body silhouettes then colour in the areas where you feel your different emotions. Use red for active areas, and blue for inactive.

Sadness

Fear

Jealousy

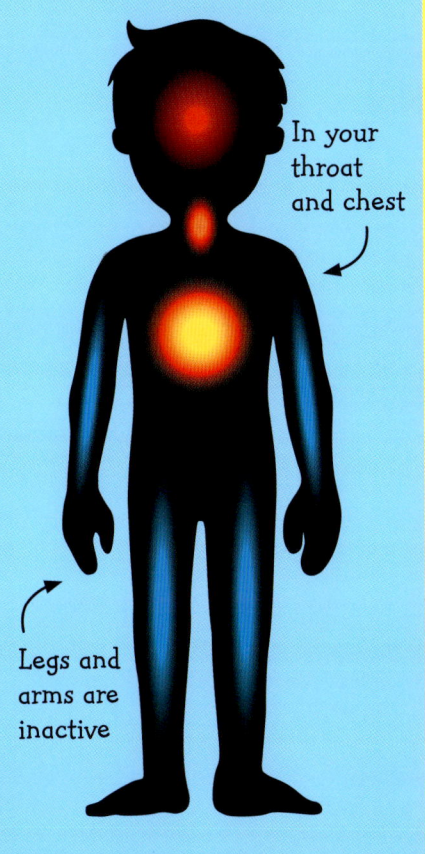

In your throat and chest

Legs and arms are inactive

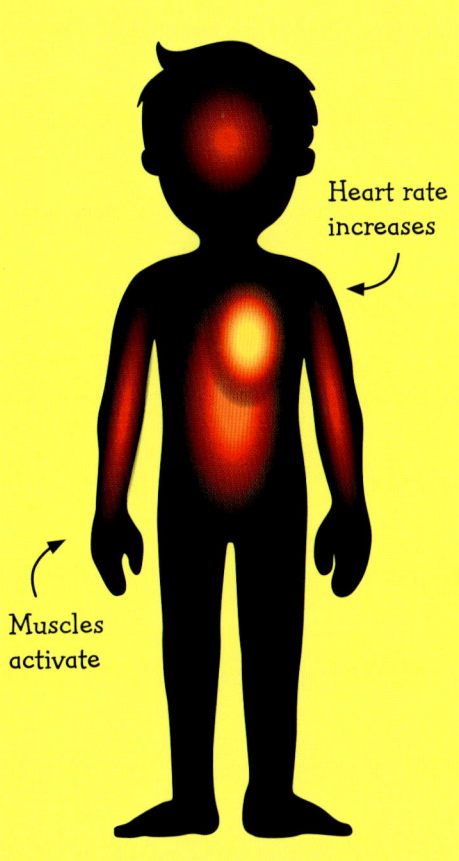

Heart rate increases

Muscles activate

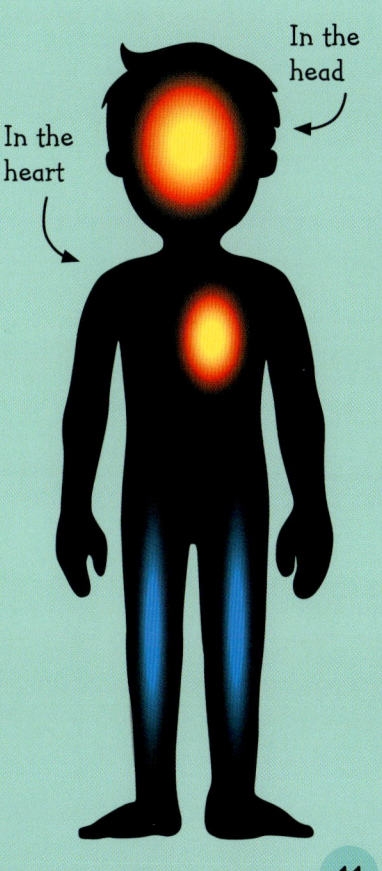

In the head

In the heart

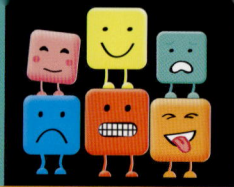

All emotions, including anger, fear, and sadness, are important. They are **natural** and make you who you are. So go ahead, **show your feelings!**

Anger

Anger helps us stand up and defend ourselves.

Emotions help us to survive

Since humans first walked the planet, our emotions have helped our survival.

Fear

Fear may tell us when it's time to run away.

It's how we deal with our emotions that matters. I get really angry when people say anger is bad. Grrr!

Without **emotions**, humans would be like **robots**.

Sadness shows other people when we need help.

Sadness

Why do we need emotions?

Emotions allow other people to understand us. They help us to know ourselves, to be real, and to connect deeply with other people.

Happiness makes us social and energetic.

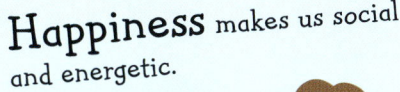

Happiness

Disgust tells us to spit out poisonous berries.

Disgust

Love helps us form strong bonds and relationships with each other.

Love

Tremendous **things** are in **store** for **you, wonderful** surprises await **you!**

Charlie and the
Chocolate Factory

Roald Dahl

What is happiness?

According to scientists, **it's four feel-good chemicals** in your **brain.**

When you smile, the happiness chemicals throw a little party in your head!

1 Dopamine floods your brain when you feel pleasure.

2 Serotonin helps keep the good feelings flowing.

3 Endorphins are feel-good chemicals, which reduce feelings of pain.

4 Oxytocin is the "cuddle" hormone, produced by hugs and kisses.

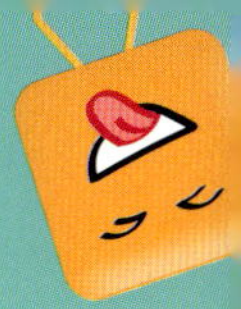

A good laugh

Laughing is the best fun exercise there is.

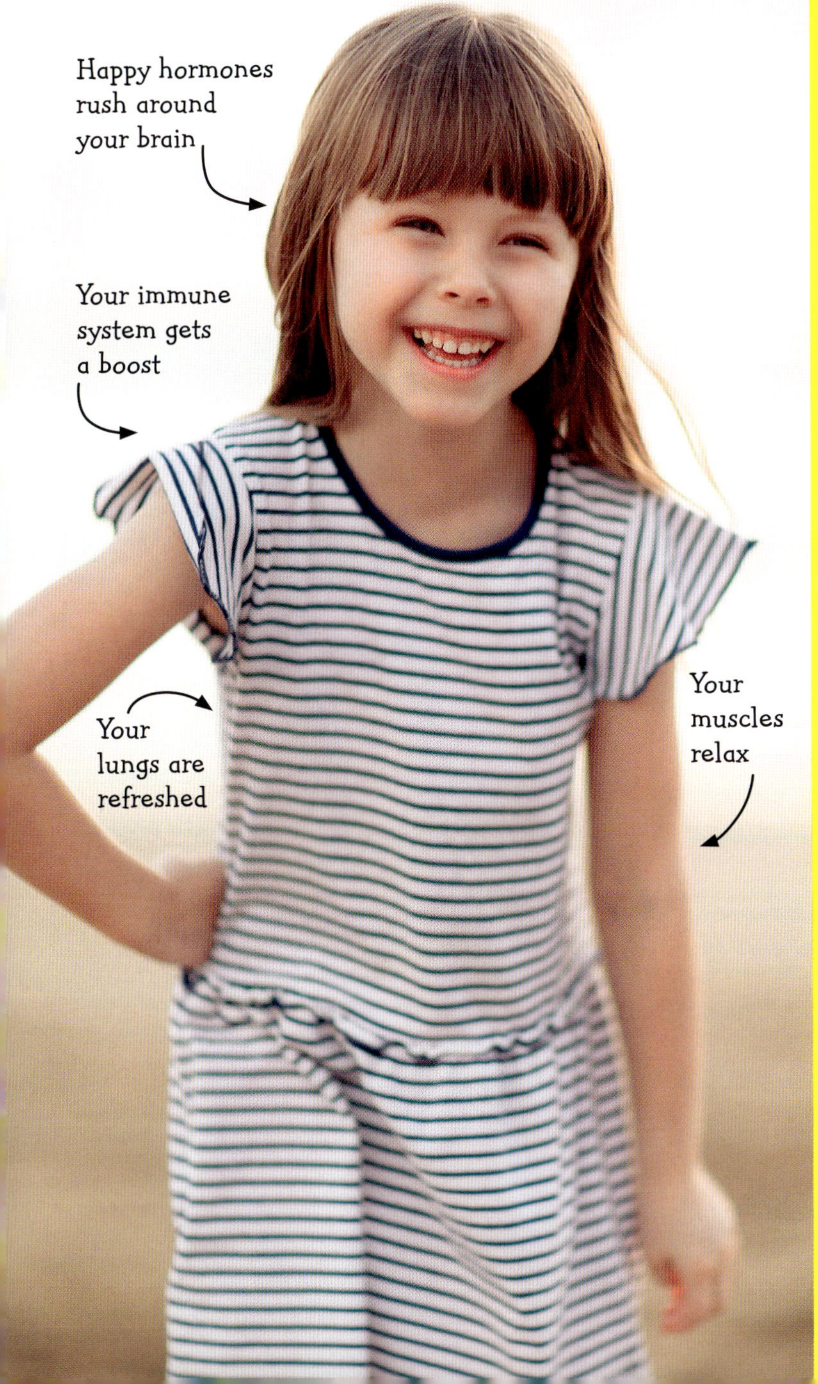

Happy hormones rush around your brain

Your immune system gets a boost

Your lungs are refreshed

Your muscles relax

The magic of happiness

Scientists have proved that happy people benefit from... more happiness!

 Because you feel better, you do better.

 You move faster – there really is a spring in your step.

 You get on better with your friends and family.

 Your body heals faster and is healthier.

 Happiness helps you cope better with stress and worry.

 You are more generous.

 Your happy energy is contagious.

A bowl of happiness

Imagine you have a big bowl, and you want to make a **happiness cake.** What do you need for the **ingredients?**

Being outside among nature

Exercising

Reflecting on happy memories

A scientist would use these ingredients. They are all proven to increase happiness chemicals.

Doing something you love – that's a type of happiness.

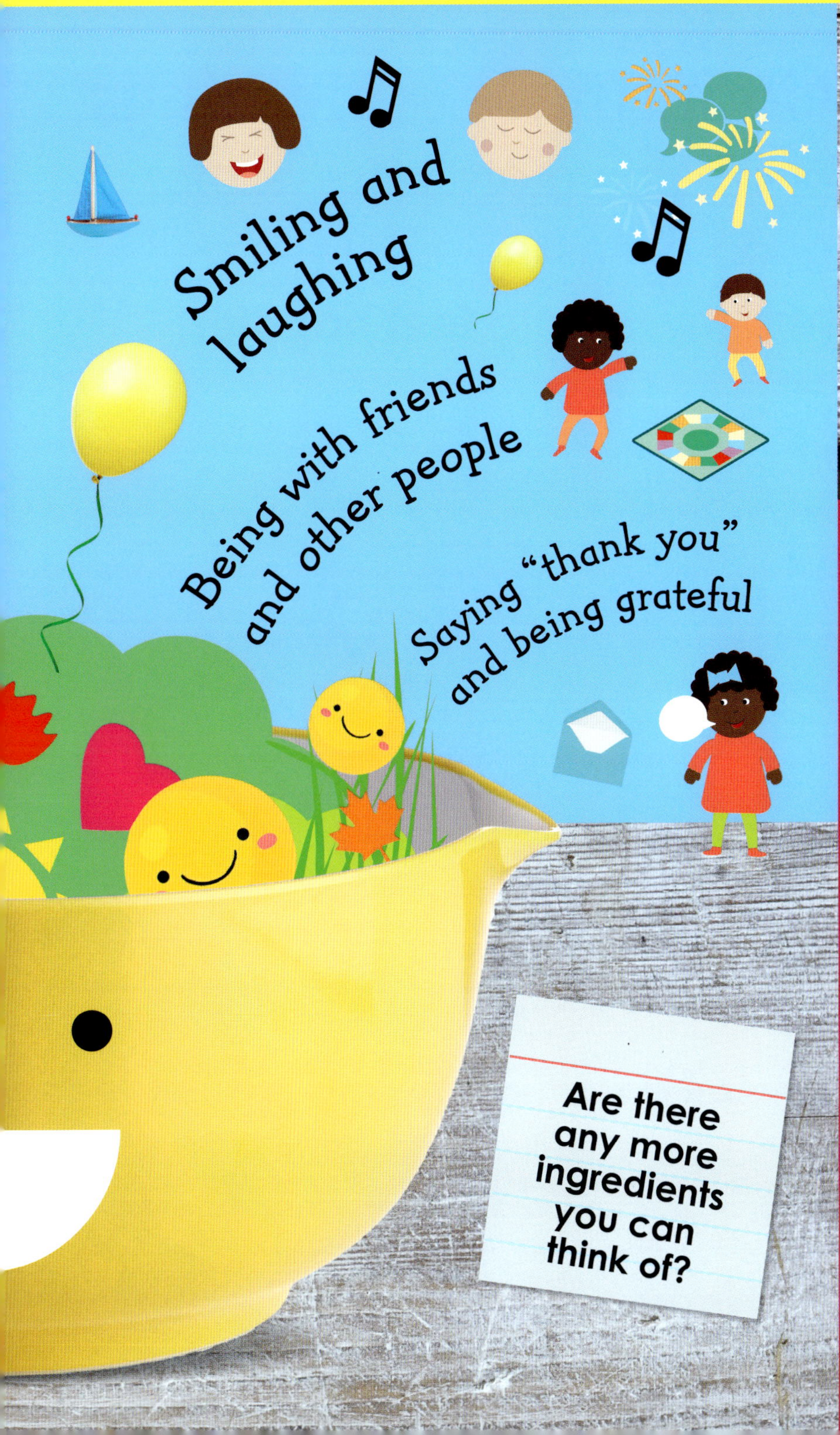
Smiling and laughing
Being with friends and other people
Saying "thank you" and being grateful
Are there any more ingredients you can think of?

Gaming

Gaming is good fun, that's for sure, but is it a good way to make happy memories? Scientists believe you could be better off and happier if you do activities with friends and family instead, so try and strike a happy balance.

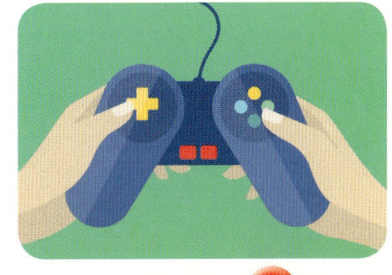

Choosing happiness

Life is like a roller-coaster – there are lots of ups and downs. A great habit to get into is to think of the good things in your life. Then make a decision, choose to be happy now!

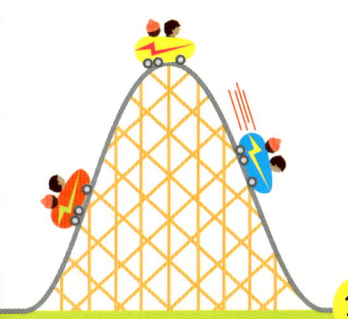

Be grateful

Hello, I'm very proud and excited to meet you. Thank you for being my friend!

Counting your blessings,

and being grateful for all the good things in your life, is a healthy way to **feel happier.**

Fine! I'm grateful!

Being grateful is not just about saying "thank you". As an emotion, gratitude is feeling thankful or appreciative. Not every day is perfect, but being grateful for things, no matter how small, will wash away anger and negative feelings, leaving you feeling happier.

Say "thank you"!

Count on one hand

To get started, begin by asking yourself, "What could I be grateful for?" and see if you get any ideas.

Look at your hand, or draw around it, and name one thing you can be grateful for on each finger.

Maybe you can go on to your other hand too...

There is a strong link between gratitude and happiness.

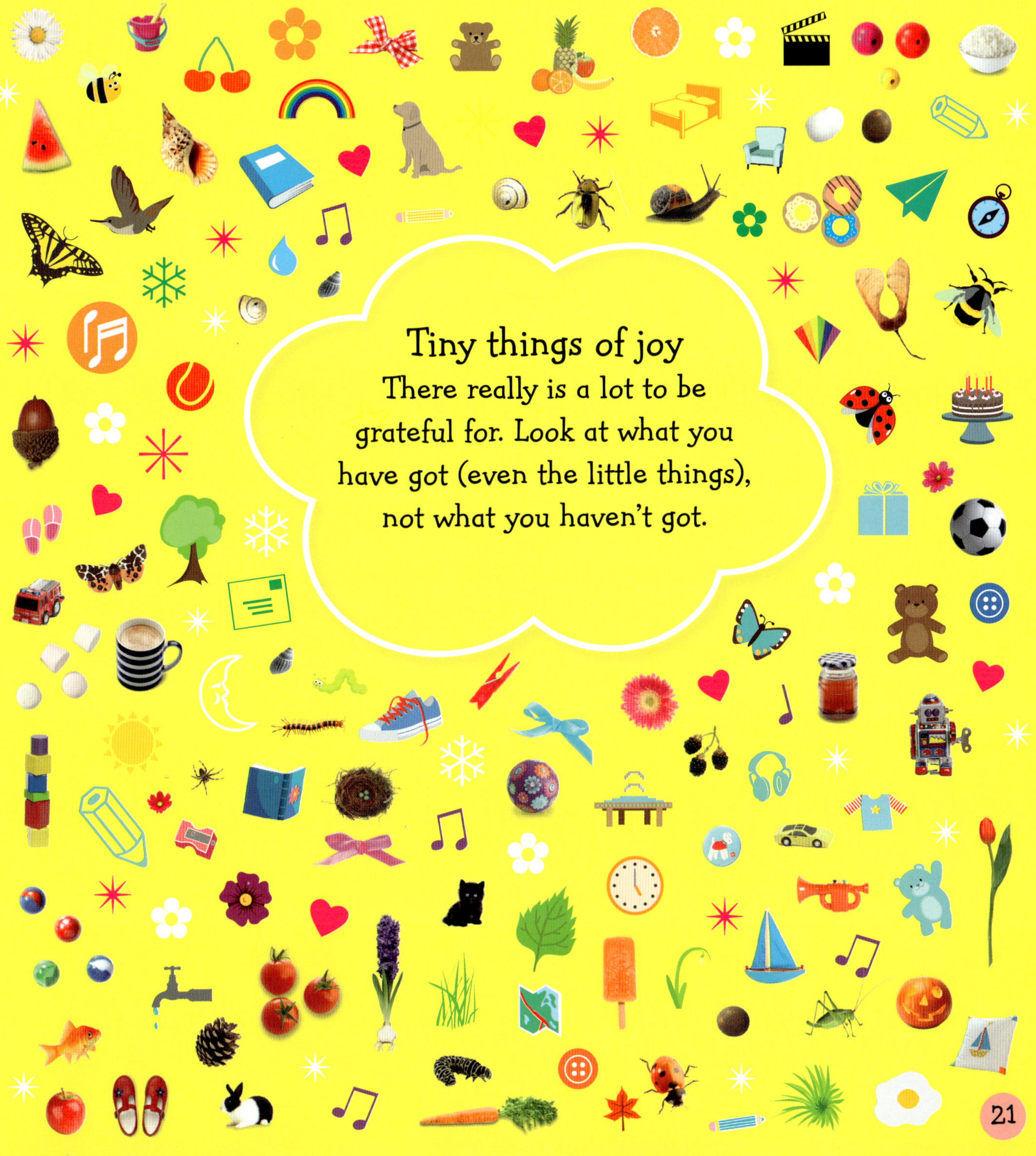

Tiny things of joy

There really is a lot to be grateful for. Look at what you have got (even the little things), not what you haven't got.

One thing you have for sure is **YOU**, so be **grateful** for the **wonderful** person **you** are.

Look at this field of flowers. Each one has a special quality. Imagine you are going to pick a bunch – and give them to yourself! Choose flowers that describe you and that you can be thankful for.

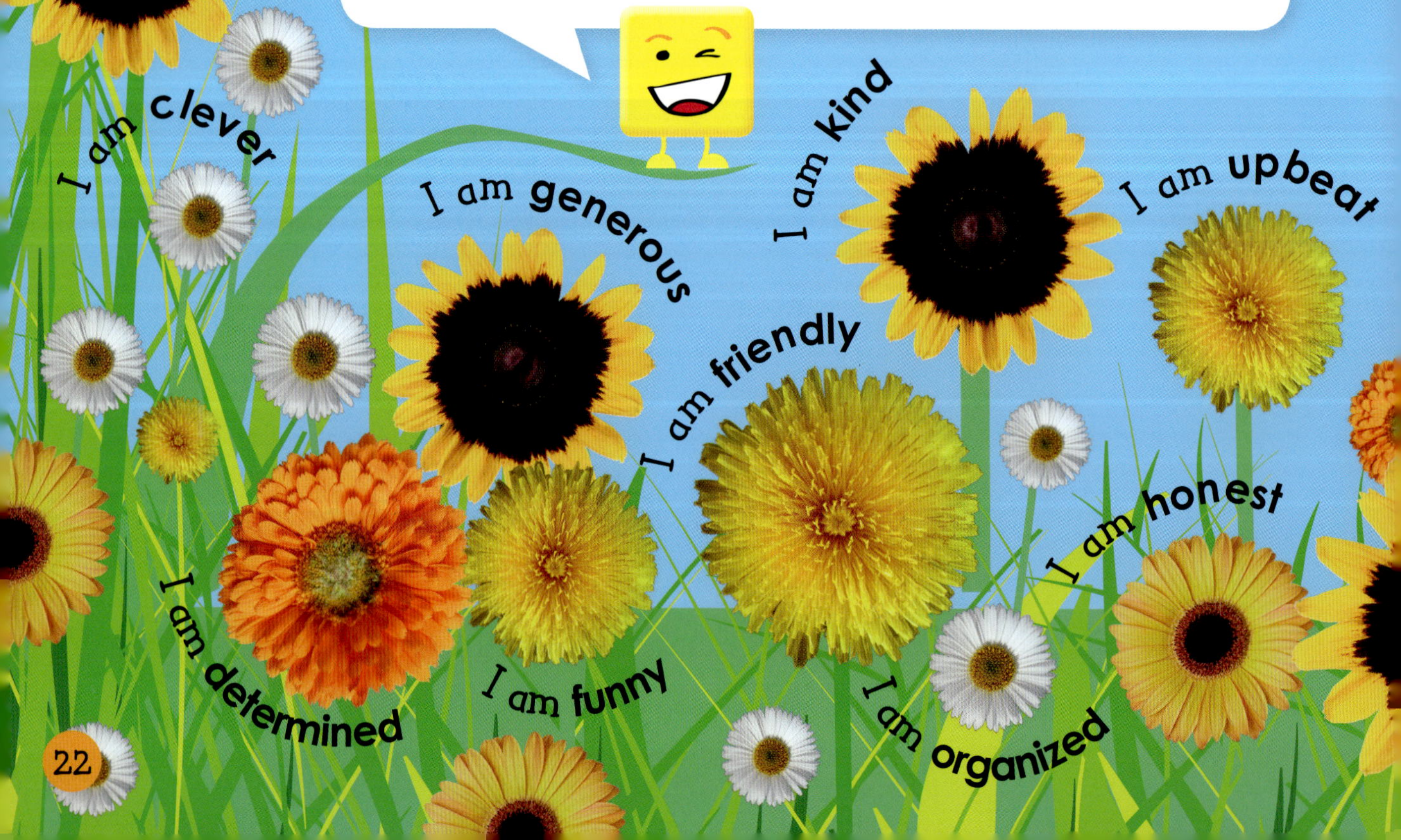

I am **caring**

I am **creative**

I am **clever**

I am **generous**

I am **kind**

I am **upbeat**

I am **friendly**

I am **honest**

I am **determined**

I am **funny**

I am **organized**

Well done you!

There are lots of **everyday achievements** to be **grateful for,** no matter how small. What have you done to be grateful for today?

- Have you shared well?
- Were you enthusiastic?
- Did you work hard?
- Did you do something brave?
- Maybe you made a funny joke?
- Were you kind to a friend?

All these are things you have done because **YOU are YOU!**

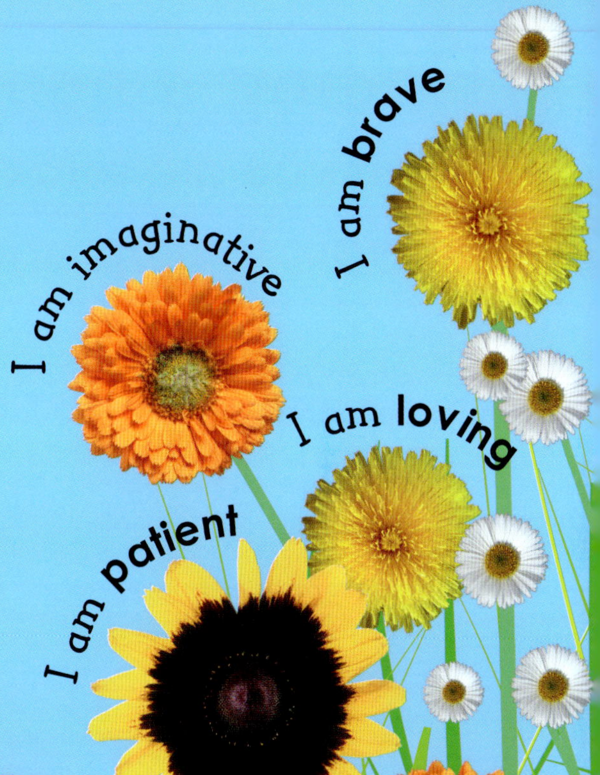

I am **brave**

I am imaginative

I am **loving**

I am **patient**

I am **playful**

I am **energetic**

I am **daring**

I am artistic

I am thoughtful

I am cheerful

I work hard

I help others

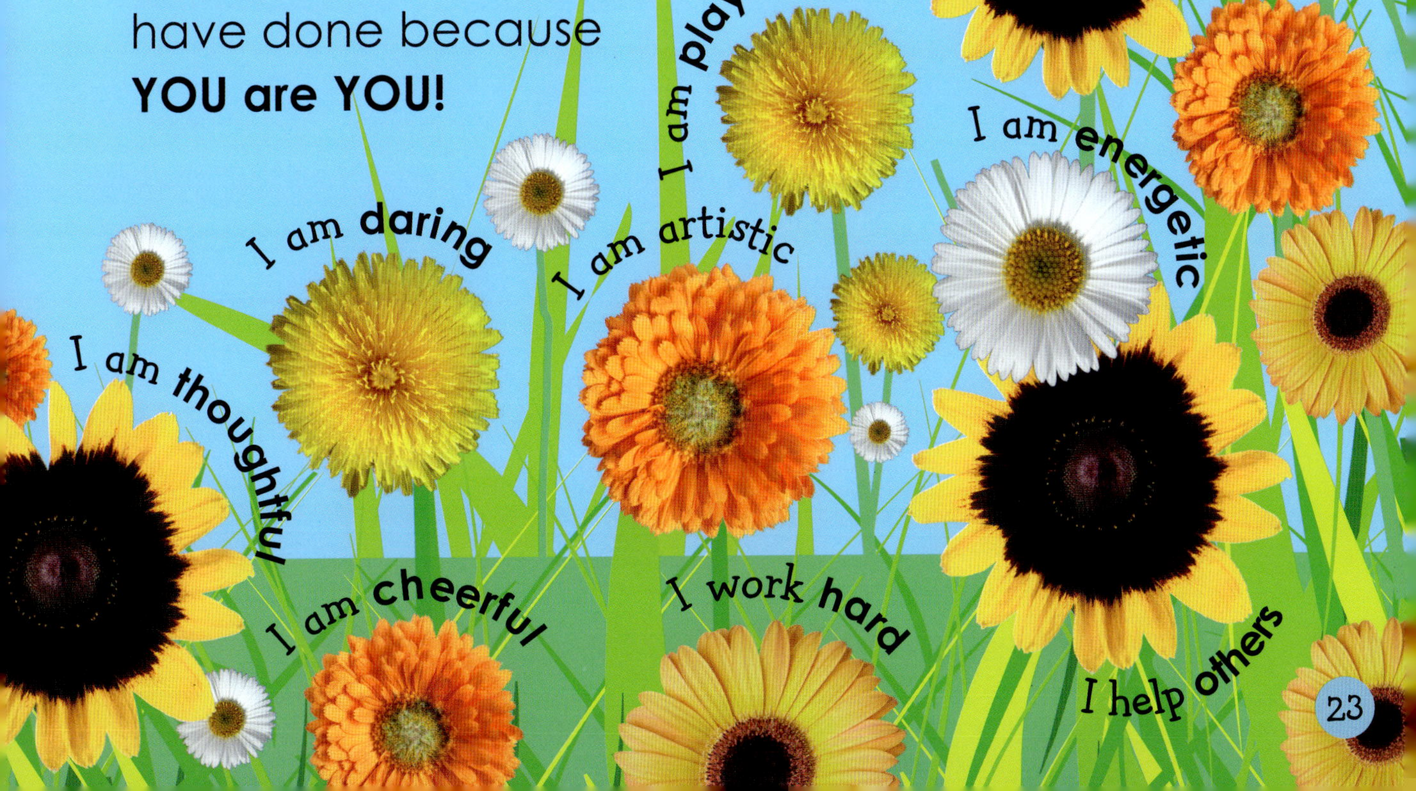

23

Finding a happy balance is easier when **you** are **relaxed** and **calm**. It's time to **put your feet up** and **take it easy**.

Here are some of the positive effects of relaxing:

Your stomach can digest food better.

Your breathing rate slows down.

Your blood pressure goes down.

Relaxing helps your body heal when you are unwell.

Your concentration and mood improve.

You'll sleep better.

Your heart beats slower.

Fewer stress hormones are released.

Your muscles ease.

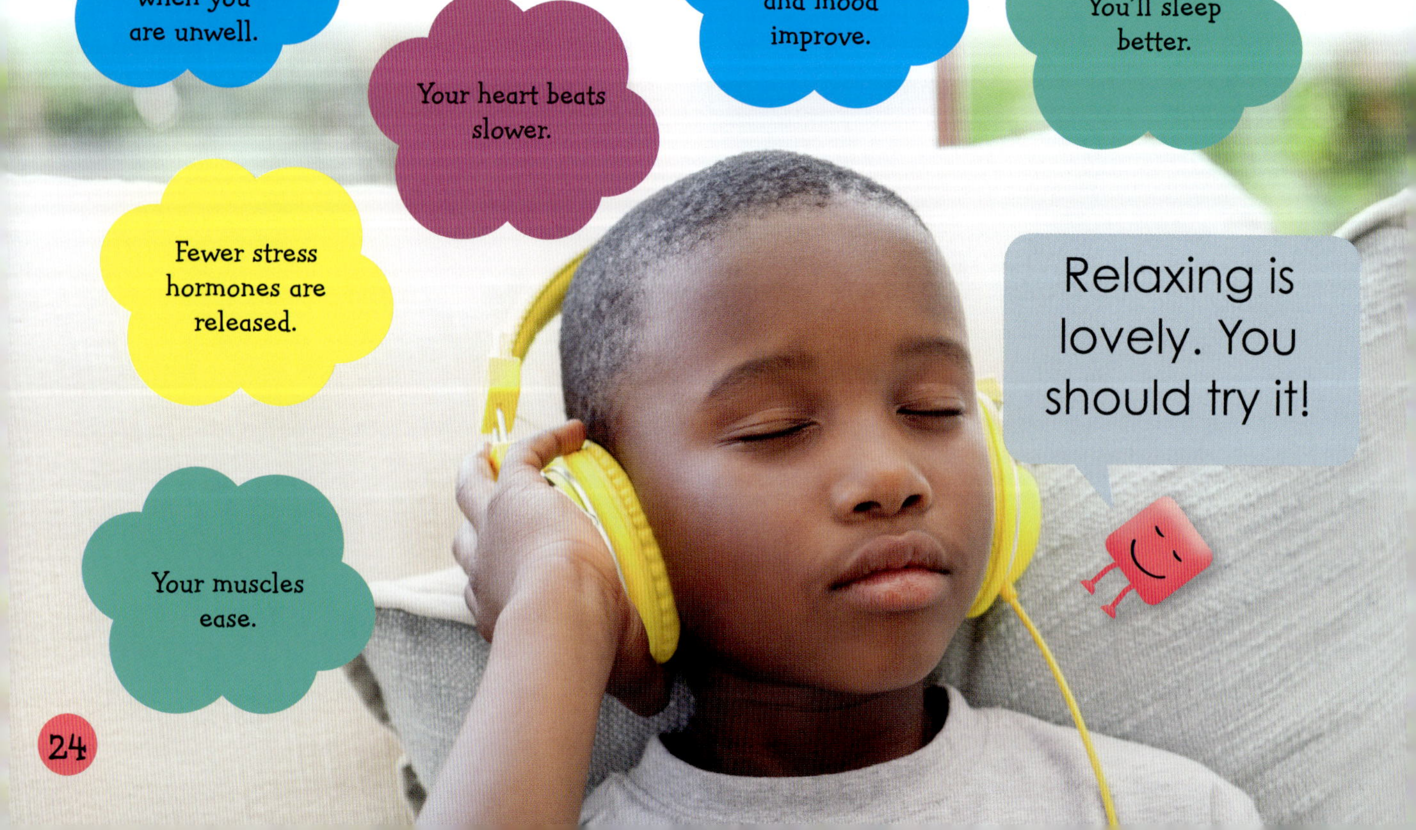

Relaxing is lovely. You should try it!

24

What do you do to relax?

Choose some activities to help you relax when you feel:

Go for a walk in the countryside

Exercise

Exhausted

Stressed

Worried

Listen to music

Have a nice warm bath

Take some deep breaths

Watch a fun film

ZZZZZ

Have a lie down

And if you don't get enough sleep, you might feel like these little fellas!

Sleep well
Sleep is very important – that's when you do your growing (it's only when you're asleep that your body produces growth hormones). Getting enough sleep also helps you feel positive and happy.

Angry

Overactive

Greedy

Irritable

Grumpy

Relax, relax

1 **Smell the flower and blow out the candle**
Breathe in through your nose for a count of four, then breathe out through your mouth for a count of four. Pretend you are smelling a flower, then blowing out a candle.

Smell *the* flower
1 2 3 4

Blow out the candle
1 2 3 4

Breathe yourself calm
These simple breathing exercises can be done anytime, anywhere.

Trace the star with your finger as you breathe.

2

Hold your breath and smile →

Deep inhale

Belly breathing
Put your hands on your tummy and feel it balloon out as you breathe in slowly and deeply through your nose.

← Deep exhale

3

Hold for two seconds

Hold for two seconds

Hold for two seconds

Breathe in

Breathe out →

Breathe out →

← Breathe in

Breathe in →

Breathe out

Breathe out

Breathe in

← Breathe out

Breathe in →

Star breathing
If you feel upset or angry, calm down with slow and gentle star breathing.

Hold for two seconds

Hold for two seconds

26

Make an arch

Try not to wobble

Bottoms up!

Arch like a cat
Shoulders over wrists, hips over knees, carve your tummy in, curl your toes. Then arch your back up and relax your head.

Flamingo balance
Shoulders back, arms out, lean forward, pick up your left foot, and flap your arms slowly. Then swap legs.

Downward dog
Head down, hands spread, tail bone pushed up, and legs straight. Make your body into an upside-down V shape.

Head high

Yoga helps with being flexible and strong as well as calm and relaxed. Try these pet-acular poses!

Twit twoo!

Hiss like a cobra
Shoulders down, neck long, hips and thighs stay on the ground with long, stretched-out legs. Hissss!

Pretend to be an owl
Sit on your heels, lay your palms on your knees. Twist your upper body one way and then the other like an owl turning its head.

What is mindfulness?

Mindfulness is a **big word** for **noticing your thoughts** and **being aware** of how your **body feels** RIGHT NOW.

It's sure to be a good day!

Animal magic

Have a go at this meditation. Sit down so you feel relaxed and tune in to your senses. Pretend you have senses as powerful as these animals...

...eyes that can see like an eagle.

...a tongue that can taste like a snake.

...ears that can hear like a bat.

...a nose that can smell like a dog.

Fingers that can feel like a spider feels vibrations.

28

A noticing walk

Make a walk into a "noticing walk". Concentrate on your senses. What do you See, Hear, Smell, Feel? Is there anything you haven't noticed before?

See – blue sky, flowers, trees, people playing games.

Hear – children playing, aeroplanes passing overhead.

Smell – grass, flowers.

Feel – warm sun, breeze blowing.

Taste – an apple.

Afterwards, draw around your hand and make a memory. Remembering with all your senses helps memories to stick in your head.

Mind yourself!
Here are some more ways to make your day extra mindful.

Before you get up – notice each part of your body in turn. Start at your toes and end at your head. How does each bit of you feel today?

Mealtimes – pay attention to and savour your food by eating it slowly, using all your senses.

Any time – practise gratitude and share with your family one or two things you are grateful for that day.

> **"**
>
> I am not **afraid** of **storms,** for I am learning how to **sail** my **ship**. **"**

Little Women

Louisa May Alcott

Seeing red

Have you ever **lost your temper?** Did you **yell** and **scream** and want to hit something? **Anger** is a healthy **emotion** that everyone feels sometimes.

Anger can help you defend yourself and change things that are unfair. It can be a force for good.

Look at these faces. Which one looks angry?

a

b

c

d

e

f

g

h

Anger prepares your body for action.

Stay in control of your anger. Don't let it control you!

Your reaction

What's happening?

STAGE 1

I heard that!

Raising the alarm
Your brain prompts your body to produce stress hormones. These make your heart beat faster so that blood is quickly pumped to your muscles. Your muscles need oxygen so you start to breathe faster.

STAGE 2

No WAY!

Power boost
The tough "fight" hormone is released to give your anger power. Your muscles tense. Your body is working hard. It starts to become hot and your face goes red.

STAGE 3

WHAT did you call me?

More and more intense
Your muscles start twitching and jerking into action. You start frowning and purse your lips together. Your pulse quickens and your palms become hot.

STAGE 4

Arghhh!

Boiling point
You speak louder and faster. Your heart starts thumping. Your cheeks go even redder. Your body tries to cool down so your veins stick out and you start to sweat. You are ready to take on a TIGER!

STAGE 5

I'm so tired.

Afterwards
Afterwards, you may feel exhausted and tearful as all your stress hormones leave your body, and you start to calm down.

Anger can be like an **iceberg.** What you see above the surface is just a **tiny part.** Most of the iceberg is **below the surface.**

GRRRRR!

anger

Sometimes it's hard to keep your cool.

Let's dive down deeper!

embarrassed

helpless   alone

stressed

guilty

trapped

nervous

jealous

frustrated

Anger is not simple! Try to get to the bottom of it by talking things through calmly with an adult.

Taming your temper

One of the hardest, and simplest, ways to control your anger is to recognize what is happening to you BEFORE you blow your top. Then you can do something about it, like simply say:

"I am angry!"

Handy tips

When you start to get **angry**, look at your **hands!**

1
Put your hands in your pockets or sit on them. This will help to restrain you.

2
Take deep breaths and blow into your hands – this is a wonderful way to calm your body quickly.

3
Ask for a hug – find someone you love and hug it out.

4
Make a fist, then relax your hand – this is a great way to remove some of the tension building up in your body.

5
Count to five – this simple tactic gives you a chance to think before you act.

That's not fair!

What is fairness?

Fairness is treating people equally. It's taking turns, telling the truth, listening with an open mind, and **owning up to mistakes**.

Fairness is one of the most important moral values in the world.

Is this fair?

If your sister gets a pair of new shoes, you may feel "that's not fair!". But your sister may NEED new shoes. Fairness isn't everyone getting the same. Fairness is everyone getting what they need when they need it.

It's not fair! Not everyone has glasses!

Not everyone NEEDS glasses.

Fair or Foul?

Where do you think these scenarios fall on the anger scale for you and other people?

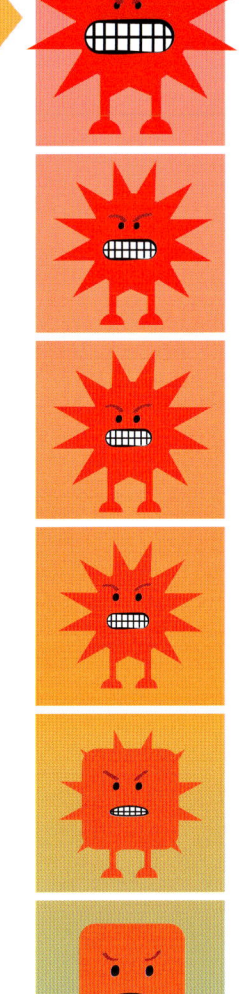

Your sister got the window seat AGAIN.

Your friend has a new toy, but won't let you play with it.

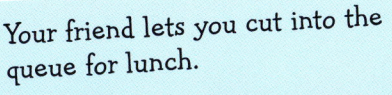
Your friend lets you cut into the queue for lunch.

You saved a seat for someone in the dining hall.

Your sister got money for her birthday and you didn't.

Your brother has gone to the cinema with your mum and you are left behind.

You might have heard grown-ups say "Life's not fair" and sometimes it might feel like that. If things don't go your way, use the techniques on the next pages to help you feel better.

Let it go

Often your **anger** is reasonable and healthy. Even so, feeling things are **not fair** is not a nice way to feel. So how can you deal with **frustration** and **anger?**

Keep cool challenge

It can be tough keeping a cool head – are you up to the challenge?

1
The first step
Recognize what's happening. Your unfair button is on red alert, your chest tightens and your thoughts are fuelling the anger.

2
Stop!
Slam on the brakes! Don't do something and get into trouble. It's never too late to change your behaviour.

3
Close your eyes
Block out what you're angry with. It will help you get back to a balanced state quicker.

4
Breathe
Remember your breathing exercises from page 26!

5
Decide
Now you are calmer, think about the best way to deal with what happened.

Imagine your frustration is an "It's not fair!" balloon. Now pretend to let it go...

It's not fair!

Your challenge

From now on, think of the "keep cool" challenge whenever you start to feel like you are losing your temper. Remember to breathe and put yourself back in control.

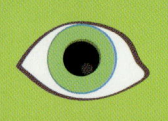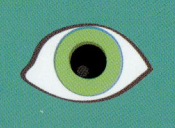

Green-eyed monster

Jealousy is a **natural human emotion** that even babies feel. But it can change a **happy, friendly person** into a green-eyed monster.

I want **that**!

What is jealousy?
Jealousy is when you feel angry and upset about what others have, or can do.

Try not to compare yourself to others

He's more popular and clever than me.

She's funnier and kinder than me.

also amazing

amazing

The green-eyed monster can creep up on the best of people. But there are not many winners in the game of comparison.

How jealousy feels
Jealousy is a mixture of anger and disgust. Your body can't help reacting.

Brain
Anger and disgust chemicals are sent out.

Eyes
You pay close attention to the person you are jealous of, and can't see other things.

Heart
Your heart quickens and blood pressure rises.

Stomach
Stress hormones course through your body, and you don't feel like eating.

Green and sneery?

The **jealousy doctor** is coming to the **rescue!**

Quick fixes

- **Repeat:** "I am enough, I have enough."
- **Think:** What are you good at?
- **Act:** What do you love doing?
- **Speak:** Say something nice.

Cure those jealous twinges

Even the best of friends can get jealous of each other at times. When you feel jealous, take some deep breaths and try to think of something you are grateful for instead.

Ooh! I'm having a twinge.

Be yourself. Everyone else is taken.

How do you feel?

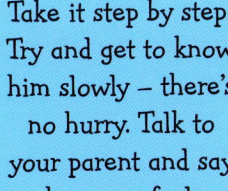

Problem	Symptoms	Remedy
 My sister gets everything. My parents show favouritism towards her!	• Fighting • Teasing • Hiding stuff • Telling tales • Name-calling	Learn to share, compromise, and say what you want. Talk about how you feel to your parents. 
 My best friend has found someone else to play with.	• Plotting revenge • Gossiping • Saying things you wish you hadn't	Focus on other children and making new friends. 
 My mum's new partner is taking my real dad's place, and taking attention away from me.	 • Being rude • Demanding attention	Take it step by step. Try and get to know him slowly – there's no hurry. Talk to your parent and say how you feel. 
Other kids are much better at things than me.	• Teasing • Put-downs • You feel like giving up	List your own talents and accept that everyone is unique. You are awesome too.

" The true **courage** is in **facing danger** when you are **afraid**, and that kind of courage **you** have in **plenty**. "

The Wonderful
Wizard of Oz

L. Frank Baum

It's hair-raising!

Meeting new people or reading out loud can be scary. **Being scared** is not a sign of weakness. **Everyone gets the jitters sometimes!**

Fight or flight?

People have felt the "fight or flight" response since the first humans walked the Earth. When a caveman was faced with a snake, he had two choices:

1 Run away = flight

2 Fight the snake = fight

Your body gets itself ready for quick action (or a quick escape).

Brain – stress hormones are released

Eyes – pupils dilate and you get tunnel vision

Hands – shake

Ears – loss of hearing

Mouth – dry

Arms – hair raises

Heart – beats faster

Skin – flushes

Muscles – tense up

Stomach – digestion slows

Bladder – relaxes

Do you worry a lot? You could have inherited this from your family.

Spot the difference

Fear and worry – people use these words for unpleasant feelings to do with being scared, but what's the difference?

Fear is the feeling of being afraid. You can feel afraid of the dark or something scary like a snake.

Worry is the feeling of concern. You can feel worried about making friends at a new school or passing your spelling test.

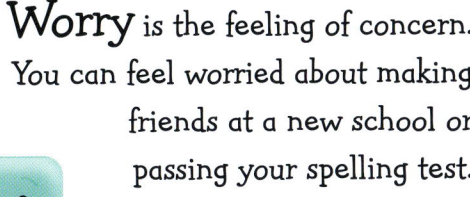

FEAR

A scared mouse
This mouse is feeling fear because there is danger nearby. Fear will make him run away.

WORRY

What if the cat comes out?

A worried mouse
This mouse is concerned there might be a cat about. He's worried.

What to do about worrying

Worrying can turn little things into **huge things.** But you **can** find the **power** to ease your worries.

Do you worry about any of these things? I worry about them all!

Worries can grow stronger and stronger as the thoughts in your head feed your fear.

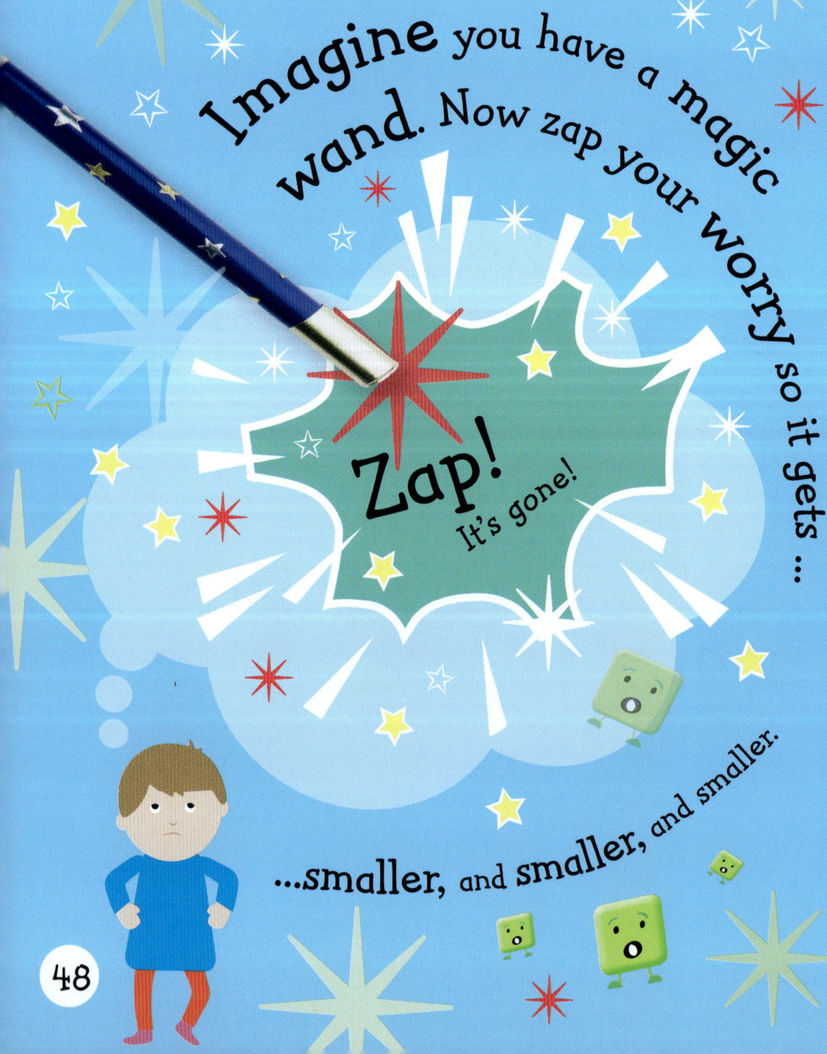

Imagine you have a magic wand. Now zap your worry so it gets ...

Zap!
It's gone!

...smaller, and smaller, and smaller.

Here are common things kids worry about

- Meeting new people
- School
- Family problems
- Something bad happening
- Falling out with friends
- Being sick at school
- Monsters and the dark
- Bullying
- Tests

Say to yourself like a mantra: "I am brave, I can do it, I am strong!"

The worry work-out

Give your worries the worry work-out, and check out page 26 for those breathing exercises too.

Help me, please!

?

1
Work it out

Sometimes it's obvious what you are worried about. Other times, it might not be. Write your worries down or whisper them to a favourite toy and work out what's really bugging you.

Some problems, like family problems or being bullied, can be big and too tough to work out alone. Skip to step 3.

2
Think it better

Switch to action mode so you feel more hopeful. Think of possible things you can do that might help with your worry. For example, if you have a worry about doing a presentation at school, practise with your family as the audience. If you are worrying about falling out with a friend, invite him or her over for tea.

If you can't think of any ways to make it better, go to step 3.

3
Ask for help

Talking through your worries with a caring friend or adult really helps. Don't keep your worries to yourself!

TELL! TELL! TELL!

A problem shared is a problem halved.

Scientists have proved that sharing your problems really does reduce stress!

Big changes in your life, like a **new school** or even having braces fitted, can feel **scary.**

Nerves are natural
Humans don't like change and scientists know why.

Do you ever feel these things when you're nervous about something?

1 Your brain has worked hard to make your old routine into a habit. It's hard to let go.

2 Your brain likes things to be certain. Anything uncertain could be a threat to your survival.

3 Change can affect our relationships. As humans naturally live in groups, anything that disrupts our social lives can be unsettling.

Headache

Trouble sleeping

Tearful

Sick

Can't make decisions

Sweaty hands

Butterflies

Tummy ache

If nothing ever changed...

Scientists call the connection between your head and your intestines **the brain-gut axis.**

Brain

If your brain is worried, it upsets the tiny microbes here.

Your body is finely balanced.

microbes can affect your brain.

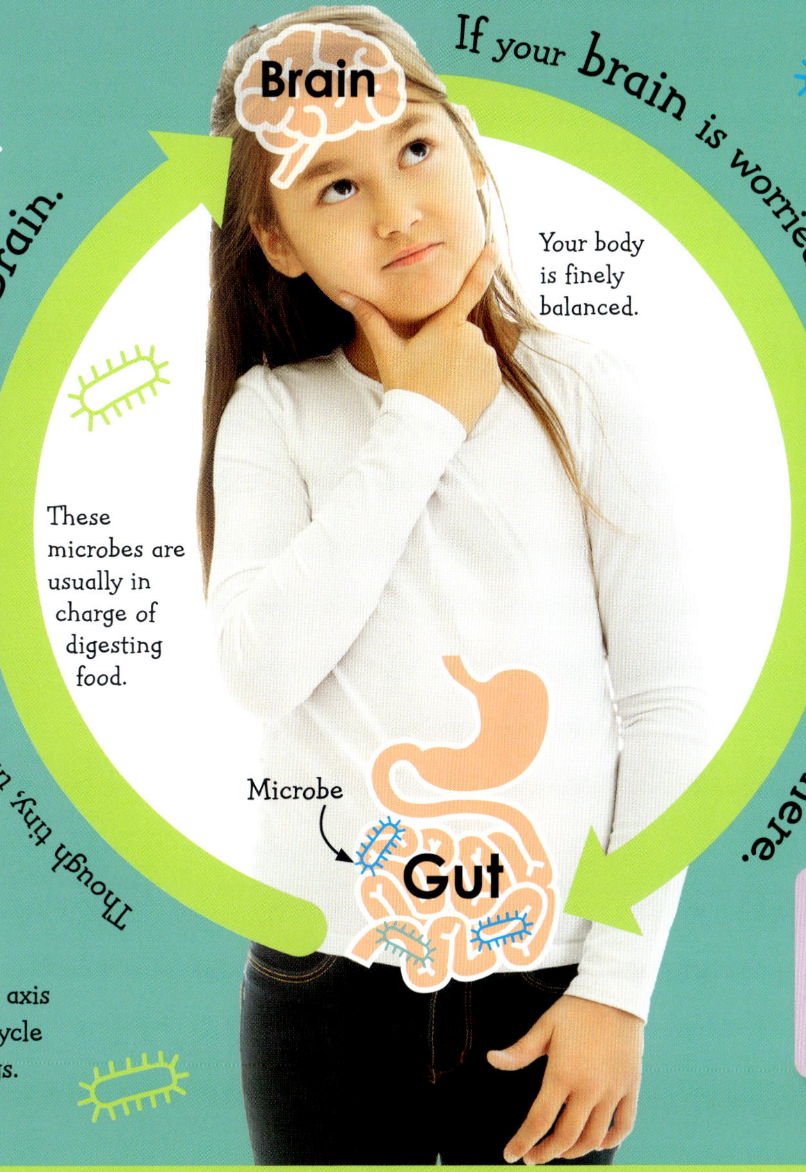

These microbes are usually in charge of digesting food.

Though tiny, the

Microbe

Gut

Most worries won't last long, and you will get used to your new challenge quickly.

The brain-gut axis can cause a cycle of sick feelings.

...there would be **no butterflies.**

51

Here are some **top tips** to ease **you** into practically **anything.**

Find out as much as you can – for example, go to a school open day and look at the school website.

Be prepared the night before, with all the right clothes ready and equipment packed.

Plan something special – for example, a packed lunch with all your favourite foods.

Remember! The school/dentist/new place knows you are NEW. You will be shown around. **There will be people to help,** and **you might even have a mentor.**

Had a bad start?
Not everything always goes right straight away and you may find the first-day jitters don't fade away immediately.

Think: "Something wonderful **is** going to happen."

Eat a healthy breakfast – good food will make you feel better and more able to cope.

Think of the good things about your new place or experience.

List the things you are looking forward to.

Talk about any worries with a caring adult so you can get reassurance.

Take a deep breath, calm down, and look at the facts coolly.

Remember times in the past when you have felt this way, and how you got through it.

If you are finding it hard to make friends, bear in mind that this can take time.

Separation and divorce

Change is a natural part of life, but when it happens to your family, it can be **hard to deal with**. If your parents decide to divorce or separate it's **important** to **talk about how you feel** and ask them for **honest answers.**

Fact 1
Kids don't cause divorce or separation.

Fact 2
Kids can't change divorce or separation.

Fact 3
Your parents still love you.

Fact 4
Your parents are still your parents.

A kid's guide to a grown-up problem

An emotional time

Here are some emotions you may feel if your parents split up.

Unhappy
You don't want your parents to live in different places.

Angry
You feel your stable home is being destroyed.

Relieved
There's been a lot of fighting recently.

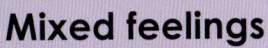

Sad
You may feel hopeless and helpless.

Mixed feelings
You might feel a mixture of all these things.

Fear
You are faced with a big change and that can be scary.

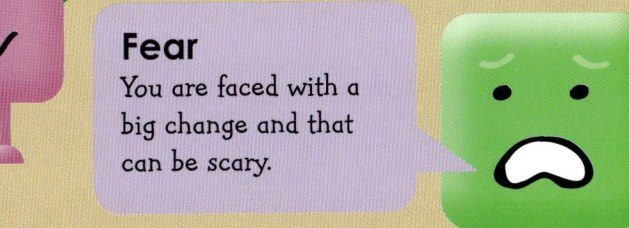

Open up!

If you find it hard to talk to your parents, find a friend or caring adult to confide in. And if one of your friend's parents are getting divorced, be a good listener. He or she is going through a tough time.

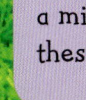

The changes split-up parents bring

may mean a **new home**, and even **a new family.**

Two homes? Here are some tips to feel at home in both of them:

Have a calendar so you can see when and where you will be.

Follow the same routines at both homes as much as you can.

Have everything you need in both homes, so you don't have to pack too often.

Give your new situation a chance.

"Hello, who are you?"
Your parent may start seeing someone new. You will need time to get to know the new adult in your life. This person is not replacing your real mum or dad. Try giving him or her a chance, and remember to talk about any issues you have with a trusted adult.

Your emotions might be up and down. Make sure you don't suffer in silence.

Ask for one-on-one time with your parent if you feel you need it.

A blended family

A blended family happens when a couple move in together, bringing their children from a previous relationship with them.

Your issues **are fair** and **right**

Most blended families report that they are happy families.

Make sure you have a space in your home that you can call your own.

It might be hard to understand what is happening, so ask lots of questions.

Do your best to get on with new step-siblings, but don't worry if it doesn't happen overnight. Things will get better with time.

"

After a **storm** comes **fair** weather, after **sorrow** comes **joy.**

"

Russian proverb

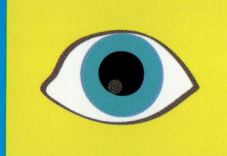

Good grief

Sadness shows other people you need **help, comfort,** and **support.**

A good cry
You need to let the sadness out to let it go. And your body helps you do that when you cry.

Frown

Watery and crying eyes

Sad voice, low, and mumbling

Crossed arms

It's natural and healthy to feel sad sometimes.

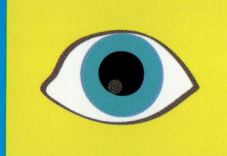

Humans are the only species to cry tears because of their feelings.

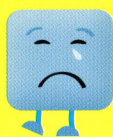

Ingredients of tears

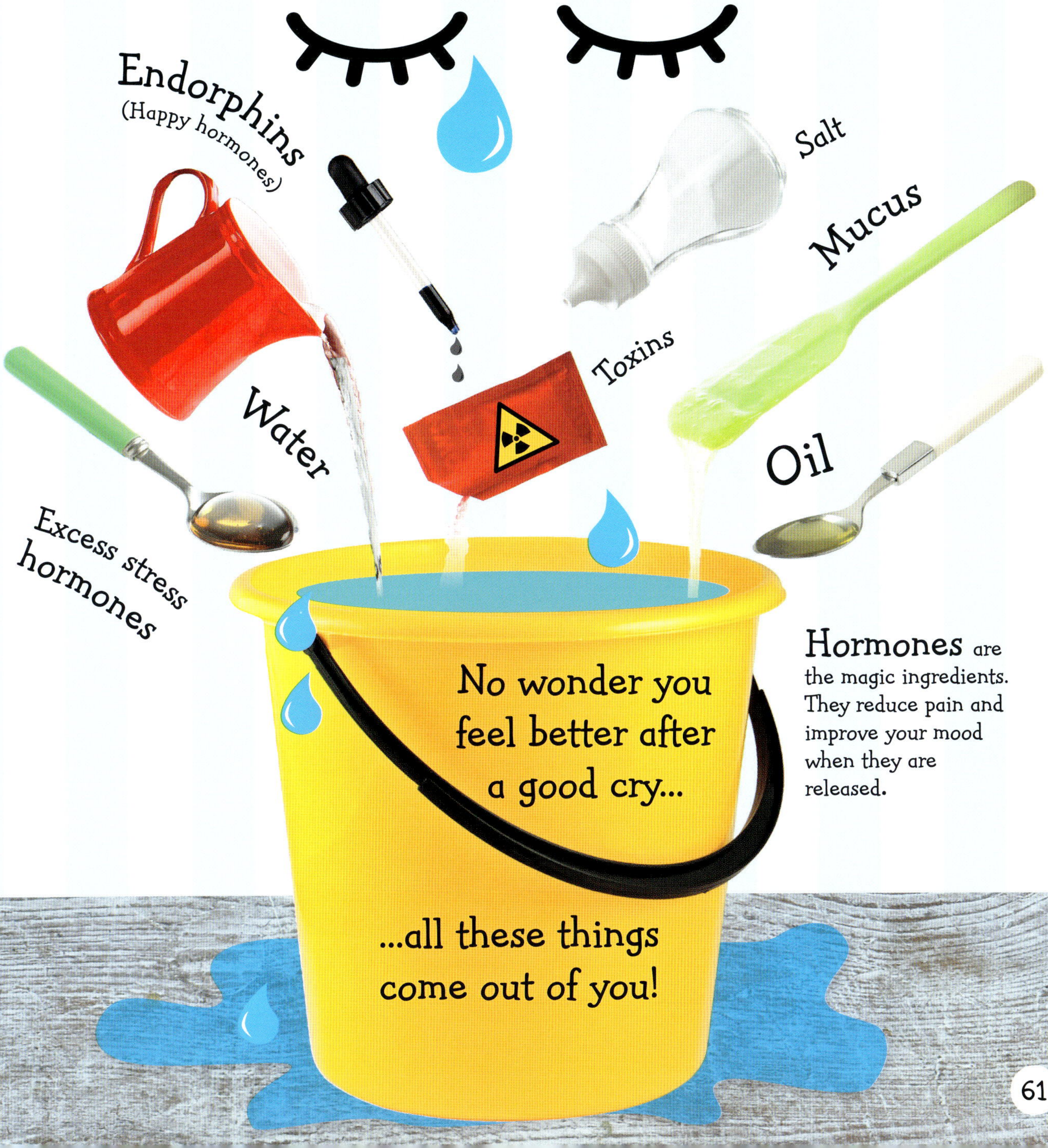
Endorphins
(Happy hormones)
Salt
Mucus
Toxins
Water
Oil
Excess stress hormones
No wonder you feel better after a good cry...
...all these things come out of you!

Hormones are the magic ingredients. They reduce pain and improve your mood when they are released.

Beat the blues

Feeling **sad** doesn't feel nice. Here are **six** sadness-busting strategies.

1

Find your happy place

Close your eyes and imagine a place where you have been really happy, like on holiday or your birthday.

Now draw your happy place!

2

Breathe yourself calm

Sit cross-legged, close your eyes, and imagine the sun is warming your face. Now do some bumble bee breathing. It's comforting, calming, and peaceful.

Then put your fingers in your ears.

Breathe in deeply through your nose, so that your chest puffs out.

Hum while you breathe out slowly through your mouth.

If you feel **sad** a lot, make sure you talk to a caring adult.

3
Calming words
Think of calming phrases such as "I'm OK", "I can cope", "It's not so terrible".

I'm OK.

It's not so terrible.

4
The big three
Write down three reasons why it is not so terrible, or three ways you can cope, or three reasons why you will be OK.

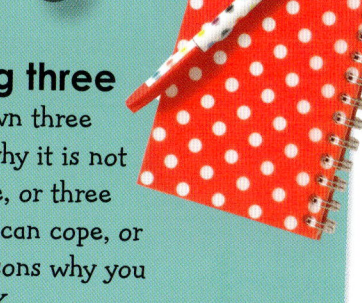

Sometimes all you need is a big hug.

5

Do something you enjoy
A change of scene or an activity you love can help bring back the joy.

6
Talk to someone about why you are sad.

Bullying damages everyone involved.
It's **time** to be **clear** about **bullying.**

What's a bully?

A bully is someone who...

...uses words to

- make threats
- spread rumours
- tease and name-call

Fact: leaving someone out of a group is one of the worse types of bullying.

...uses strength to

- kick, hit, push, or trip
- take or break someone's belongings
- scare someone else on purpose

...hurts by

- excluding someone from a group
- telling other children not to be friends with someone
- embarrassing someone on purpose

Where does it happen?

Travelling to and from school.

At school.

On the Internet and at home.

What it feels like to be bullied

- You feel you can do nothing to stop it.

- You may feel smaller and weaker than the bully.

- You feel outnumbered and helpless – there are more of them.

- It may feel confusing, you don't know why someone is being mean.

- It feels like there is nobody to talk to or stand up for you.

- You feel very sad and alone.

**BUT there is help.
Turn over to find out more.**

You have the **right** to **feel safe** at **all times.**

Bullying is NEVER acceptable.

Here is helpful **advice** for **everyone** involved.

What to do if someone is **bullying you...**

Tell someone you trust. If it is easier, write the person a note.

Never keep being bullied a secret. Keep on telling people until someone does something about it.

Avoid areas where the bully feels comfortable picking on you, like places where teachers can't see you.

If you can, **surround yourself with friends** and people who will stand up for you.

People to tell: parents, teachers, the headteacher, playground mentors, or older friends. You will get help.

What to do if you **see someone** who is **being bullied:**

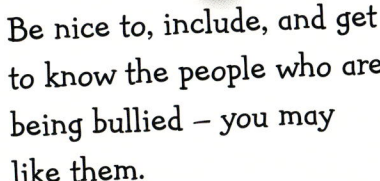

Don't cheer the bully on or **stand around** to **watch.**

Try to make friends with the bully too – show them they don't need to bully others to be accepted or cool.

Be nice to, include, and get to know the people who are being bullied – you may like them.

If you see someone **being bullied, find someone to help stop it.**

First of all, stop and think!

What to do if **you are** a **bully...**

Think of the damage you are doing and hurt you are causing.

Find another outlet (such as sport) for your aggressive feelings.

Talk to a school **counsellor** or **caring adult** if you are having problems.

Bullies are more likely to be in trouble when they are older, as well as get into trouble now. So stop!

67

I don't fit in!

Feeling **"different"** or that you don't fit in can make you feel **sad and alone.** But **everyone is unique,** and **you are too!** There's nothing different about that.

Many children who feel "different" turn out to be successful.

Be yourself! You're the best at that.

Albert Einstein didn't fit in at school, and one of his tutors called him a "lazy dog"! He never wore socks – even when he was invited to the White House for dinner! As an adult, he became one of the most famous and brilliant scientists in history.

Finding friends
You have as much right to be happy as anyone else, so if you feel left out or that you don't fit in...

• ask your teacher to help. They are usually good at pairing kids up

• join a club to find friends with similar interests

It's important to **believe** in yourself.

Practise these friendship skills

Be friendly

Listen

Share

Say nice things

Offer your help

Be kind

Keep secrets and confidences

69

Why do pets die?

A pet quickly becomes a member of the family and a best friend. Sadly, animals do not live as long as humans, and the joy of having one can turn to heartbreak when they die.

The natural cycle of life
Pets may die of old age, illness, or an accident. Death is a part of life, so enjoy and care for your pet during the precious time you have together.

I'm Monty! I loved playing with my ball.

Five sad stages
When you lose a loved pet, you may feel any of these five things, in any order.

You can't believe it
You may find it hard to accept what has happened, and feel numb. You may even deny that your beloved pet has died.

It makes you angry
You may think what has happened is unfair, and try to place blame. You may think of a time you were mean to your pet and blame yourself.

Your love for your pet will never die – he or she will live forever in your memory.

I'm Betty! I loved kissing my friend.

I'm Harry! I loved stuffing my cheeks full.

Saying goodbye

As a family, it's nice to say a final goodbye to your pet. You could have a ceremony, write a letter or poem, or plant a tree. Honouring your lost pet will help you move on.

I'm Moppet! I loved lying in the sun.

You make deals

You may make little bargains, like "if today is sunny, it won't be true". This is normal too. Death is very hard to accept.

You feel very sad

You might start to feel very sad and that you want to be on your own to cry and grieve. It's OK to cry!

You accept it

You will eventually come to terms with your loss and find you're able to think of the good times you and your pet had together.

Today you are you.
That is truer than true.
There is no one alive
who is youer than you!

Happy Birthday to You!

Dr. Seuss

73

Whatever you **do,** whatever you **think** or **feel,** you are **unique** and **awesome** – in fact, you are a **wonder** of nature.

Every single snowflake

These are unique things about you, even among 7.6 billion people!

Yours and yours alone

Your beliefs

Your personality

Your ear shape

Your irises (the coloured part of your eye)

Your tongue's bumps and ridges

Your voice

Your toe prints and fingerprints

Your DNA (the genetic formula that tells your cells how to build you)

is unique – just like you!

You can do it!

Believing you can do something

is half the battle. If you **believe** you can **work hard** and improve, **you will** work hard and **improve**.

The growth mindset

- I can learn anything I want to.

- I keep going when I'm finding it hard.

- This will take time but I will keep going.

- I learn from mistakes.

- I will do my best.

- I like a challenge.

- I believe in myself.

If I can think like this, I can achieve anything.
Let's go!

Step by step

Some things might be an uphill struggle, but it'll be worth the climb.

I did it!

I will do it.

I won't do it.

I can do it.

I can't do it.

I'll try to do it.

I want to do it.

How do I do it?

No one is perfect. Everyone makes mistakes, so give yourself a break! Celebrate your differences, share your similarities, and believe in yourself.

Life is a journey...

...enjoy the ride!

My emotions dictionary

These words can help you explain how you feel.

Sad

Blue – Generally sad.

Disappointed – Upset because something is not as you thought it would be.

Gloomy – Everything is darker than usual.

Grumpy – In a bad, sad mood.

Heartbroken – Extremely sad, like your heart is breaking in two.

Helpless – When you feel there is no one to help you.

Hopeless – When you feel there is no hope.

Mopey – Floppy and sad.

Tearful – You want to cry or you are crying.

Upset – Unhappy, like you could cry.

Happy

Contented – Happy and satisfied.

Delighted – Extremely happy.

Enthusiastic – You like it a lot and you are very interested in it.

Excited – You are enthusiastic and eager.

Fulfilled – You have everything you need.

Funny – Like you can make good jokes.

Glowing – So contented you feel you are glowing.

Joyful – Full of joy, very happy.

Love – To like a LOT.

Merry – Smiley and cheerful.

Proud – Pleased with something you've done.

Angry

Annoyed – Something or someone is making you quite angry.

Boiling point – About to get really cross.

Cross – A bit angry.

Envious – Resentful, usually because you want something someone else has.

Frustrated – You feel you haven't got what you want or need.

Furious – Extremely angry.

Fuming – So angry, like steam is coming out of your ears.

Irritated – Something is winding you up.

Jealous – Angry and resentful.

Scared

Anxious – You are worried something is going to happen that will be scary.

Fearful – Full of fear.

Jittery – Jumpy with nerves.

Nervous – Edgy, jumpy, and worried.

Panicked – Out of control with fear.

Petrified – So scared you can't move.

Shocked – Stunned, dazed, and upset.

Stressed – Worried and frazzled.

Tense – Your muscles have tensed up, your jaw is clenched, and you're worried.

Terrified – Scared stiff.

Worried – Concerned and anxious.

All mixed up?

It's possible to feel happy and sad at the same time, or scared and excited, or grumpy and funny. You can take words from any column, or add ones of your own.

Glossary

Activate – To make something active.

Anxiety – A feeling of worry about something that you are unsure about.

Chemical – A type of substance.

Concentration – Complete attention.

Digest – To break down food in your tummy.

Divorce – The legal ending of a marriage by a court of law.

Dopamine – A messenger chemical in the brain.

Emotion – A strong feeling, e.g., sadness, anger, or joy.

Endorphin – A chemical released by your brain that can reduce pain.

Gratitude – The quality of being thankful.

Hippocampus – The centre of emotion and memory in your brain.

Hormone – A substance in your blood that rouses you to do things.

Hypothalamus – A region at the front of your brain.

Issue – A personal problem or difficulty.

Mantra – A statement or slogan you chant over and over.

Meditation – When you focus your mind for a period of time in silence or with chanting to relax.

Microbe – A tiny bacterium in your gut.

Mindfulness – When you focus on the present moment, and at the same time calmly notice your feelings, thoughts, and five senses.

Nerves – Feelings of nervousness.

Oxytocin – A hormone, sometimes called the "cuddle hormone", as it increases when you get a hug.

Prefrontal cortex – The very front of your brain.

Prey – An animal that is hunted by another animal.

Relax – When you relax, you become less tense and anxious about things.

Scientist – A person who has studied and become an expert in science.

Serotonin – A chemical in your brain that helps good feelings flow.

Stomach – Your tummy, where food is digested.

Stress – Mental or emotional strain or tension.

Survive – To continue to live.

Symptom – A sign that something that is not good exists.

Thalamus – Either of a pair of two areas of grey matter in your brain. They act like a switchboard.

Yoga – Certain spiritual body poses with breath control that people do for health and relaxation.

Index

A

adults, confiding in 49, 53, 55, 56, 66, 67

anger 7, 10, 12, 30–43, 55
  feeling things are unfair 36–37, 38, 39
  healthy anger 12, 32, 38
  keeping cool 35, 38–39
  signs and stages 33

B

believing in yourself 76–77
blended families 56–57
body
  feeling different emotions 10–11
brain
  chemicals 16
breathing exercises 26, 38, 62
bullying 64–67

C

crying 60, 61

D

"different", feeling 68–69
disgust 10, 13, 41
divorce or separation 54–57
dopamine 16

E

endorphins 16, 61

F

fairness 36–37, 38, 39
fear 7, 8–9, 11, 12, 44–57
  family changes 54–57
  signs of 46, 50
  worrying 47–49
friendship 69

G

gratitude, practising 20–23, 29

H

happiness 7, 10, 13, 14–29, 62
  chilling out 24–27
  ingredients 18–19
hippocampus 8, 9
hypothalamus 8, 9

J

jealousy 11, 40–43

L

laughing 17, 19

M

mindfulness 28–29

N

nerves 50, 51
new experiences, dealing with 50–53

O

oxytocin 16

P

pet, death of a 70–71
prefrontal cortex 8, 9
professional help 5

R

relaxing 24–27

S

sadness 7, 11, 13, 55, 58–71
  being bullied 64–67
  crying 60, 61
  sadness-busting strategies 62–63
  signs of 60
serotonin 16
sleep 25
stress hormones 9, 24, 41, 46
survival, emotions and 12–13

T

thalamus 8

U

uniqueness of you 68, 72–75

W

worrying 47–49

Y

yoga 27

Acknowledgements

The publisher would like to thank the following for their kind permission to reproduce their photographs:

(Key: a-above; b-below/bottom; c-centre; f-far; l-left; r-right; t-top)

10 123RF.com: Iryna Bezianova / bezyanova (b). **11 123RF. com:** Iryna Bezianova / bezyanova (bl, br, bc). **14 123RF. com:** Choreograph. **16 123RF.com:** Alexassault (bc). **17 Alamy Stock Photo:** Folio Images (l). **21 123RF.com:** Bartkowski (cb). **Dorling Kindersley:** Natural History Museum, London (fcl); Stephen Oliver (cb/Ice lolly). **Dreamstime.com:** Tracy Decourcy / Rimglow (bc); Vaeenma (br). **24 123RF.com:** Wavebreak Media Ltd (b). **28 Dreamstime.com:** Nataliia Prokofyeva / Valiza14 (b). **29 123RF.com:** michaeljayfoto (cb); Roman Sigaev (t). **Dreamstime.com:** Glinn (crb/Grass); Mikhail Kokhanchikov / Mik122 (crb); Larshallstrom (b). **30-31 Depositphotos Inc:** GeraKTV (t). **30 123RF.com:** Sergey Oganesov / ensiferum. **32 123RF.com:** alhovik (tl); Wang Tom (clb); Hyunsu Kim (cb); Ion Chiosea (bc). **34 Dreamstime.com:** Leonello Calvetti / Leocalvett. **38 123RF.com:** Janek Sergejev (c). **39 123RF.com:** Roman Sigaev. **41 iStockphoto.com:** EvgeniiAnd. **42 123RF.com:** Micha Klootwijk (Background); Cora Müller (b). **44 123RF.com:** Yarruta. **46 Depositphotos Inc:** Maxximmm1 (br). **Dreamstime.com:** Glinn (clb, bl). **47 123RF.com:** michaeljayfoto (cb/Grass border); Roman Sigaev (c). **Dreamstime.com:** Glinn (cb). **48 Dreamstime. com:** Zokad182g (tl). **51 Dreamstime.com:** Piotr Marcinski / B-d-s (c). **52-53 Dreamstime.com:** Larshallstrom (b). **54 123RF.com:** Maksym Bondarchuk / tiler84 (crb); Nontawat Boonmun / porstock (cb); Julia Moyceenko / juliza09 (cb/Violets pot); Denys Kurylow / denyshutter (b). **54-55 123RF.com:** Roman Sigaev (t). **Dreamstime.com:** Glinn (Background). **55 123RF.com:** jessmine (bc/Purple watering can); Alexander Morozov (bc). **56 123RF.com:** syntika82 (tl, bc). **57 123RF.com:** syntika82 (cra). **58 123RF. com:** lucadp. **60 123RF.com:** Anurak Ponapatimet. **61 Dreamstime.com:** Andrey Eremin / Mbongo (bc). **64 123RF.com:** Valeriy Lebedev (Shadow); Wavebreak Media Ltd (br). **66-67 Dreamstime.com:** Larshallstrom. **69 Alamy Stock Photo:** Alpha Historica (tl). **Dreamstime. com:** Larshallstrom (r). **70 123RF.com:** Csanad Kiss / vauvau (crb). **71 123RF.com:** Antonio Gravante (cl). **74-75 123RF.com:** sxwx (t). **74 123RF.com:** Pteshka. **75 Alamy Stock Photo:** F1online digitale Bildagentur GmbH. **76 Alamy Stock Photo:** Hero Images Inc.. **79 123RF.com:** Roman Sigaev

All other images © Dorling Kindersley

DK would also like to thank:
Marie Lorimer for indexing, Caroline Hunt for proofreading, and Ben Patané for design assistance.